Love & War

A STORY OF TRAGEDY AND TRIUMPH

Tia Becca

Love & War: A Story of Tragedy and Triumph

Copyright © 2016 by Tia Becca

All rights reserved. No part of this book may be reproduced or transmitted in any form or by any means without written permission of the author.

ISBN: 978-0-9916015-4-7

Published by:

This book is dedicated to Jordan, my first true love.

Contents

Introduction 1
Preface. 5
1 Dear Mama. 7
2 Cigarette Burns. 13
3 Grown-Ass Child 19
4 Bees in the Trap 29
5 ATL Shawty 41
6 Sin City. 45
7 Blood, Sweat & Tears 51
8 Born Again 63
9 The Lily of the Valley. 67
10 My Own Flesh & Blood 73
11 Not Easily Broken. 83
12 My First Love 87
Conclusion 91
About the Author 97

Introduction

My name is T, but you probably know me as Tia Becca. My journey towards becoming the celebrity that you see on television is what some might refer to as triumphant. Trust me, you will read my story in disbelief. Life has thrown me so many curveballs that I wasn't even sure if I had the endurance to survive, but I have. I've decided to come face to face with the pain that has held my heart captive for so many years for several reasons, but the most important reason is to heal someone else's broken heart. I know that there is someone in the world walking through the same hell that I did, and I want them to know that this too shall pass. I share my story because I know from experience that if it has not killed you, you now have the power to be stronger. I also believe that my story reveals so many truths that people are afraid to speak on, but I'm not afraid nor have I ever been.

Like the Sade song, "This is No Ordinary Love." Nothing about my life up to this point has been ordinary. While most little girls have memories of dressing up as princesses and being treated like royalty, my childhood memories are tainted with the harsh realities of drugs, violence, bloodshed, poverty, and abuse.

Quite frankly, I never stood a chance at having a life that would lead to anything other than destruction, and that is exactly what happened.

I was born to a mother who was addicted to drugs, and it was all downhill from there. I sought love and anything that remotely felt like it because for so long, I was deprived of it. I sought love from men and often received many things, but love was not one of them. My perception of men is still skewed today, and maybe that is because, as I write to you, I still haven't found the right one.

In hindsight, the men in my life have been a tremendous part of my journey as well. Whether through positive or negative situations, they have influenced who I was, who I am, and who I will be. I decided to leave their names to your imagination and refer to them as initials. Their names are not important, but the lessons that I learned from each of them are where the hidden treasures lie.

The difference between me and many people is that I acknowledge that everything that has happened to me was either a hand that life dealt me or a bad choice that I made. That's one of the things I am most proud of: I recognize the error in my ways and how they have affected my life adversely. But I'm still standing. I want for someone reading my story to recognize that we are not who we used to be; rather, we are who we decide to become, and even if we have made poor choices, we do not have to be defined by them. With every passing moment, we have the power to change the course of our lives and right our past mistakes.

As you read these pages that I have poured my heart into, I don't want you to feel sorry for me. I only want you to learn and be inspired. Every face has a story, and we must all play the game of life with the cards we have been dealt. I believe that a story untold is equivalent to death. Today, I choose life, healing, and power. This is Love & War: A Story of Tragedy and Triumph.

Preface

Standing in line waiting to be handed a block of cheese, powdered doughnuts, and a white box of wheat cereal can do wonders for your self-esteem. I really don't know if you've ever waited for a handout, but it is a very demeaning experience. Waiting in that line to me was equivalent to the world telling us that we were not enough and that we didn't matter. This was never my ideal of living, and even though I had not seen anything different, I knew that I did not like the way it made me feel. I dreamed of the families that were on TV. Shows like Full House and The Cosby Show were fairytales to me. I really never believed that people lived like they did.

There were many days at my grandmother's home that I skipped breakfast and waited until I got to school because I couldn't bear the thought of eating that shit the government gave us. It was shit. We all deserved better. Impoverished and starved were adjectives that defined the backdrop of my life. Furthermore, my grandmother was under so much stress that our house was unkempt. The constant sight of roaches scurrying across the countertop and mice running in and out of our home made me sick to my stomach. Stacks of clean and dirty laundry mixed together, mildew around the bathroom, and that disgusting line around the bathroom tub left me in a constant state of turmoil. Life felt like an uphill battle.

There was no relief at school because other kids recognize when you don't have, so our poverty was no secret. Sometimes, I would try to sneak away to my next door neighbor's house just to eat with her family because their house was clean. It's hard for me to describe my anguish, but it felt like torture. To make matters worse, my birth mother was in and out of our lives further contributing to my feelings of worthlessness. It was just fucked up. And while I know that every face has a story and that we are all products of what has happened to us in our lives, I believe that my journey hardened my heart and instilled a stronghold that would never allow me to love. Without love, there is no real purpose for life. It feels like I spent an eternity trying to search for mine. Life has not been easy for me, but along the way, I have learned that what doesn't kill you will make you stronger.

CHAPTER I

Dear Mama

Sacrifice looks like my mama. She was really my grandmother, but we called her mama. The real truth is that she was the only mother that I knew. I watched my mother come in and out of our home too many times to count. I guess the drugs had a hold on her that was stronger than her love for us. It killed me that she didn't find us to be worthy of her love, and I felt it deep down in my soul.

There was always a silent sense of pain that was evident throughout my entire family. The weight of caring for me and my sisters and brother was bringing my grandmother to a breaking point. I could see the weariness and desperation in her eyes. Have you ever seen someone whose eyes were bloodshot from drinking alcohol excessively? Her eyes bled, but there was no alcohol, only stress. I guess after having her only daughter diagnosed with cancer at the age of three only to watch her die a slow death at age six and a son murdered in the violent streets of Dayton, Ohio, enough was enough. His case was never solved, and her heart could never find peace. Because of my mother, she was now faced with the challenge of my brother who was a crack baby. Maybe things would have been different, but the constant bouts of crying and screaming were almost unbearable. Sometimes she would have to put him in a room, close the door, and make us all stand outside for hours until it would stop. He couldn't help it; he was going through withdrawal. Have you ever witnessed someone going through withdrawal? It was fucking hard to watch because there's nothing that you can do. And after a while, your nerves are shot from the cries. We all did what we could to be there for him, but as kids ourselves, it was hard. Like I said, this ain't no ordinary love.

Things always got worse when my real mother would promise to do better. Every moment that we spent with her was like a gamble, but we kept on losing. There are countless stories of this song and dance where she would promise my grandmother that she was going to do right by us and fail. I remember it like it was yesterday when she asked my grandmother if she could spend the day with us at the park. Like usual, she swore up and down that she needed to spend some quality time with us. Against her better judgement and more than likely in need of a break, my grandmother allowed us to go. As we drove in the car, I still remember the view from the window in the front seat, and even though I could barely see out of the window, I always remembered that everything looked so dull. It seemed like the sun never shined where we lived. We pulled up to a neighborhood that looked familiar, and my mother told us that she had to run inside to meet a friend and would be right back.

As we sat in the car with anticipation, minutes turned into hours. There was nothing for us to do in the car, and just as the boredom and restlessness began to reach another level, the neighbor came out of her house and walked over to the car.

"How long y'all been sitting out here?" she said. "Here, y'all, take this change so that the next time the ice cream truck comes by you can get you something." You could see the disgust on her face because she knew that my mother's abandonment was unjust. Time continued to pass, and the ice cream truck never came. We would have given anything to hear the sweet sound of the melody that the truck plays. It builds your anticipation, and even if for only a moment, we could have touched happiness. As I sat there, I put my quarter in my mouth because I had nothing else to do. Before I knew it, my sister sitting directly behind me kicked my seat, and the quarter got lodged in my throat.

I couldn't breathe and began to fight for air and my life. All I could hear was my sister yelling, "Somebody help us. Please somebody help us." Finally, my other sister got out of the car and banged profusely on the door of the lady who had given us the money, and she came out yelling and screaming, "Get this child some help. She's turning blue." The lady ran into the house where my mother had been all along to find her.

It turns out that my mother had been inside smoking crack. She was too high to care that my life was on the line. I couldn't make this shit up if I tried. She couldn't stop getting high long enough to come and check on me.

My heart broke with sadness when I recognized that drugs had more value than her own flesh and blood. It was because of the neighbor that the man who owned the crack house threw her out. I guess you can see why my grandmother never trusted her with us. I guess you can see why I will never call her mama. According to normal circumstances, let's just say, I never had one.

And just like every other pain that my life has brought to me, I swept this under the rug as well. I've heard it stated that every rose needs the rain sometimes, but in my case, it seemed like the rain never stopped falling.

The thought of knowing that I was alone and unloved by the very person whose womb I was nurtured in was equivalent to a bullet through my heart.

And the day that I heard gunshots ring out at my grandmother's home, I knew, we had all reached the point of no return. My sisters and I sat in the window crying, screaming, pleading, and holding each other as tightly as we could as my grandmother pulled the trigger several times unloading bullets that had my mother's name on them. The shots rang out so loudly that they frightened us beyond measure.

Even our bodies next to each other offered us a sense of security. I later found out that mother had been stealing from us again. How could she steal from us when we had so little? I mean, who steals from their children to feed their addictions?

Like I said, this ain't no ordinary love.

CHAPTER 2

Cigarette Burns

A nd every time we cried from the pain of his penis penetrating our underage, underdeveloped vaginas, he threatened to hurt us even worse.

W was my uncle but he never treated us like family. He was at war and we were fighting a battle that the rest of the world knew nothing about.

I laid next to my sister on the bed while he raped and tormented her, waiting for my turn. I had no idea how badly it would hurt. There is no question why I can't trust or attach myself to people. The first people that should have loved and protected me didn't. My family was on a path to destruction, and I was front and center.

I'm not sure how molestation begins for everyone else, but ours started with my uncle coming into the bedroom and putting his fingers in our panties. Over time, he began to penetrate us on a regular basis. I still can't understand why. To this day, I remember the royal blue bedspread that he used to cover up our faces and the stench of saliva. He used to suck his thumb, and he always smelled like spit. The smell of spit today makes me nauseated. I still can't kiss a man because of him. I can't get those images out of my soul. He took away everything and left us empty. The pain from penetration felt like someone ripping my insides out. The constant in and out motion made me feel so worthless. As his body moved in and out of mine, I felt the sweat from his stomach on my chest. He was so much bigger than me. When he penetrated me, I felt my vagina rip. I could hear him breathing heavily, and I tried to block it out by visualizing those families on TV. If only I could have lived like them, maybe I wouldn't be here. I had no idea at the time where the blood came from, but now I know. As they say, if you do a thing long enough it becomes a habit. I guess over time, I got used to him penetrating me and my sister too. We didn't scream or yell as loudly. As time passed and it became regular, we could both lay there silently. The tears no longer flowed, but inside I felt like I was dying a slow death, and I know that she did too.

After W would rape us, we would run out of the room screaming and yelling and he would smoke a cigarette.

One day, I recall running away from the room so fast that I could have hurt myself. I was so devastated. No one was there to save us, and I was terrified of what else he was capable of doing. It seemed like he had so much hatred in his heart for us. I ran towards my grandmother's couch, and I remember hiding behind the couch close to a window where a white curtain was hanging. That white curtain looked like a field of clouds to me. I couldn't get to it fast enough. I felt like W was still chasing me. He wasn't, but the terror from what he had done to us was on my trail. When I finally made it down the hallway to the white curtain, I sat there in fear and in pain and in disbelief. I couldn't have been hiding because I was panting too loud. I just needed to be saved. And although I heard footsteps coming down the hall, I couldn't hold my cry any longer. As soon as I let out my first sigh, my uncle reached over the couch where I sat, placing his arm between the white curtain and the couch, and put his cigarette out on my back. The burn was unbearable, and I yelled out in pain. I could smell my skin burn. He told me if I told anyone that he would burn me again. With tears rolling down my face, I remembered how to be silent. I still have that fucking mark on my back from the burn.

When the pain of abandonment and abuse became too much for both of us to bear, the silence transformed into the whistle that blows from the tea kettle. We couldn't contain our pain any longer.

One day, my sister and I mustered up the guts to tell my grandmother what W had been doing to us. I can't imagine how it hurt her soul. After losing her other son to the violence of the streets and the unresolved circumstances of his death looming, my uncle was her only son left. He was her angel, her miracle baby and her ray of light. I carried a sentiment of guilt knowing that she would now be forced to deal with this. She flat out asked him in front of us and of course, he denied it. He even convinced us to deny it in front of her, and we became the liars. Isn't it funny how as women when we are the victims we are always under attack?

At least after my grandmother confronted him, it stopped for a while. We at least had a sense of freedom from the slavery of his sexual abuse at the hands of W.

My sister and I let this pain steal many of the best years of our lives. I walked around with my heart filled with war, not love. I harbored so much hatred and resentment towards him, and I think my biological mother as well because she was never there to protect us. This type of pain can kill you if you let it. When I turned twenty-six, I returned home to Ohio and decided to confront him. I had learned over the years that he was also molesting my cousin. I needed to get this off of my chest. The hurt that he caused was like the weight of an elephant. It took my breath away when I thought about what he had done to us. I had to muster up the strength and stick up for everyone that he had hurt so deeply. The lion in me was ready for war. I have never been a punk. Unfortunately, his countless acts of molestation had robbed me of my innocence before I even knew what was happening. Of course, he denied it, and several of our family members were angered by my decision to resurrect this family demon. Even my cousin was hurt as a result of my actions. She was angry that she had to face this again. She would later thank me for sticking up to him and admit that she needed to free herself from the torment that she had been plagued by for so many years.

That's the problem though. There are so many little girls having their souls and bodies taken advantage of, and people keep sweeping it under the rug like it never happened. That's why so many people are walking around fucked up. I don't care what anyone says, you are never right after you are forced to endure that type of trauma. You might be able to move forward in life, but that shit hurts you to your core. And let's not forget the little boys who are abused that turn into grown-ass men who can't seem to get it together. People are out here screaming for help, and the people who should be helping them, protecting them, and having their backs—family—are the main ones causing the pain. Sick, twisted bastards. W even had a girlfriend who had a daughter, and it wouldn't surprise me if he has done the same things to her. I feel so helpless that I didn't stand by the truth when we told our grandmother. I feel so powerless, like I let other people down. Maybe I could have stopped him from laying his nasty hands on another little girl if I had been braver. I will never forgive myself for that. Never.

When someone robs you of your purity, it makes you question everything. By far, I'm not gay, but I do feel more attracted to women. I know that I don't ever want to be married or in a long term relationship with a woman, but I must admit, I am attracted to them. If I had to theorize, I would venture to say that men have caused me so much pain, I find comfort in women. Furthermore, I still seek love from the mom I never had. Sometimes I feel so fucked up and empty. It occurred to me that I have never heard her tell me that she was proud of me. No matter what I have accomplished or what I overcame, she has deprived me of those words that every child longs to hear. Because of this void, things would continue to spiral even further out of control.

CHAPTER 3

Grown-Ass Child

You know shit is fucked up when your first underage sexual encounter is in an abandoned house.

Around age twelve, we went to live with my biological mother. To this day, I don't know why we went, but I would venture to say that her promises of a better life, family time, and togetherness were among my ultimate desires. I think all of my siblings wanted to experience real family life, like we saw on TV. Although my grandmother loved us with everything inside of her, she could not give us that. I knew that deep down my uncle, her only living son, hated us because we took up space in his home and took love from his mother that he believed was rightfully his.

Living with her was nothing like we expected and definitely not what she promised. We went from being children who were cared for to being babysitters. We had to babysit our younger siblings, and my mother was always gone. She was always gone. I'm certain that she was working to provide for us, and I recognize how hard that is, but I couldn't help but resent her. I have always resented her. Whereas my grandmother cared for us, my mother did not. We had to take care of ourselves, and I hated her for that. I felt like she owed us a childhood, but we always came up short.

The inconsistency of moving from place to place began to wear on me. I was tired of feeling displaced, and that feeling would plague me for years to come. We moved so often that it became second nature to us. One summer, we relocated to a house near the projects. We lived on a street called St. Agnes. With each move, I became sure about what I did and did not want for my life even at a very young age.

I recognize now that the spirit of war has always lived inside of me. I felt the need to be a hero and stand up for others and myself; maybe that girl was developing because she had been smothered for so many years. On St. Agnes, I had no problem letting niggas have it in my front yard. I would fight just for fun, and I was good at it. I guess you could say that I was a tomboy. Living back at my grandmother's house, I always felt so helpless, but that was changing. Every opportunity that I was given to prove that I was boss bitch, I did. You know what's sad though?

I don't believe that I had anything more constructive to do with my time.

Kids would come to our yard and hang out. I can't even lie: having so many people around brought me hints of joy. I enjoyed being able to laugh and just kick it with people who were just like us. We never celebrated birthdays or holidays as Jehovah's Witnesses, so there were so many things that were important to others that we were taught not to value. Even today, I forget people's birthdays because I never learned to make a big deal of them. But the laughter was so good for us. We would crack jokes and do the silly things that kids did. I enjoyed every moment. One of my sister's friends had a cousin that would come by from time to time. I called him A. I could tell that he liked me and for me; he showed me a type of affection that I hadn't seen before. One day, A told me to come with him to an abandoned house. I was too naive to realize that entering that house with him would mean that I wouldn't leave the same. We had unprotected sex because I was too afraid to tell him no. He was older than me, and I guess he knew more about what we were doing than I did. When I left that house, I was a grown-ass child.

I wouldn't exactly call it rape because it wasn't completely forced. I was just really too young to know any better. I knew that I was receiving some attention that I hadn't experienced before, and I liked it. I liked the way that it felt. I guess I was in need of anything that resembled love. And I knew for certain that what my uncle had done to us was not love. I also knew that what we were getting from my mother did not feel like love. But this was something different. I liked the way A made me feel when I was around him.

After I left that house, I knew that I wasn't the same, but I couldn't quite determine how. A few weeks later, my older sister noticed that my period never came and insisted that I take a pregnancy test. I told her, "I think I'm pregnant." I remember her dragging me to Planned Parenthood where the lady there informed us that my test was positive. Immediately, my sister said, "We need to tell Mom."

When we left, I had no plans of telling my mother because I couldn't imagine how negatively she might react. As time passed, I recognized that this was not going away, and I was left with no other option other than to divulge the fact that I was with child. When I mustered up the nerve to tell her, I sat on the bed as my mother and stepfather argued. It was almost as if I wasn't even sitting there. I felt like I was having an out-of-body experience. I was just a child still in search of a childhood. I will never forget the look on my stepfather's face. He was beyond concerned. "She's just a child; she can't have a baby. She needs an abortion," he said.

If I hadn't been so afraid of my mother, I would have voiced the pain and suffering. I would have told her that I didn't think that I could go through with it. I honestly didn't think that I had the strength. In the midst of the silence, her voice emerged: "She got herself into this. She gon' have that baby." And while I knew that everyone in the room knew that me bringing life into the world would be a struggle, my mother, a devout Jehovah's Witness, did not believe in abortion.

We would find ourselves uprooted again but this time to a cul-de-sac in a suburban community. My pregnancy was growing more and more unacceptable in the eyes of others by the day. The scrutiny was deafening. Although we didn't have much, we lived in the suburbs, and this was a step up from the projects that cultivated our souls. Even so, there were no fourteen-year-olds walking around pregnant. I was an eyesore to the entire community. In school, people would call me names like ho and slut. I would hear people speaking behind my back, "She must be real fast," or, "She is just a child." Even though I acted like it didn't bother me, it did. My age and my life didn't add up. I was uncomfortable, tired, ashamed, and tired. My mother did not make matters any better. She made it her business to ensure that I experienced every discomfort that pregnancy would encompass. She would often say, "You gon' see what this feels like so you don't do this again." By the time I reached the third trimester, I had had more than I could take. I began receiving academic services at my home. I also had a nurse that would come by to check on me. She would sit with me and talk to me and teach me what she could about caring for a child. The learning curve for me was tremendous. I wasn't interested in being a mother; I wanted to be a kid. I wanted to do the things that fourteen-year-olds did. My mental state was not healthy, and although I didn't call it by name, I was plagued by depression. So much had been taken from me during those agonizing moments of molestation. I still couldn't see the sun. It seemed like it never shined, at least not in my life.

One day after sitting around the house, my oldest sister decided to go to Blockbuster to rent some movies. Before Netflix and chill, there was Blockbuster. The aisles were filled with thousands of movie titles divided into sections by genre. I remember walking each aisle with my sister and feeling so uncomfortable. I was in pain, but as usual, I knew to disregard it. My mother had already told me that I was going to experience it all, and I would never let her know it, but today, I was in pain. As we walked through the aisles, I heard one of the ladies at the counter whisper to her co-worker, "That little girl is pregnant." The co-worker responded by saying, "She looks like she is in labor."

It turns out that a perfect stranger could recognize my situation better than me or my family for that matter. I was so accustomed to dealing with pain and discomfort that I didn't even stop recognize that my body was preparing to bring forth new life into the world.

My sister took me to my mother's home, and I labored there for hours. I can still hear my mother's voice: "I bet you want to scream, don't you?" And there in the midst of the agonizing pain, all I could think about was escaping to the white curtain that was in my grandmother's house. The sight of that curtain blowing in the breeze was symbolic for freedom, escape, purity. That white curtain represented the innocence that was taken from me then, and the memory of it was a forewarning to the innocence that I knew would be lost after I gave birth to the baby. I would soon be a grown-ass child.

"I bet you want to scream, don't you? Go on. You can scream. That child is too stubborn to scream. I bet she doing everything she can not to scream just to prove me wrong." These were the words that my mother uttered as I struggled to maintain my composure during the pain.

After arriving at the hospital, the nurses informed my family that I would not be able to receive any pain medication. I was seven centimeters dilated. No wonder I had felt the hands of death around my neck. Now, at age fourteen, I had labored like an adult woman with no help.

As soon as it was time for me to push, I gave it all that I had. I remember thinking that I had not come this far to give up now. The spirit of a fighter has always been in the very fabric of my soul. When I gave birth to my first baby boy, I knew immediately that I had transferred that same spirit to him. And even though I didn't know how, I knew that his life would be blessed.

But no matter how much of a fighter that you are, life will knock the hell out of you. After delivering my baby, I began to lose blood at an alarming rate. Shortly after the delivery, I tried to stand in an attempt to go to the restroom and I fainted. The impact from hitting my head was horrific. I was losing blood such that the doctors grew extremely concerned and ordered blood transfusions. I heard my mother refuse them. As a devout Jehovah's Witnesses, it was against our faith to receive blood from the body of another. And although every detail of our lives might not have mirrored our faith, there was never a question as to what we believed and what governed our ethics.

After bringing the baby home, I quickly realized that my mother was not going to let me be a mother to my child. I don't know if I resented her or secretly welcomed the opportunity to escape the duties of motherhood. She would chastise my every action. I couldn't change the diaper correctly, hold the bottle the way that she saw fit, or even rock him without her consent. Over time, I was like fuck it. Deep down inside, I wanted to do what fourteen-year-olds did. She always held the baby over my head like a cloud: "You need to have your ass at home and take care of this baby." But I wanted to go the basketball games and school dances, and even when I attempted to take him with me, she wouldn't allow it. I couldn't do shit. I felt paralyzed. Eventually, she took over, and my child became my sibling. To this day, she has raised him. This has created so many emotional voids in my heart. But what I valued the most was that I recognized that she had every intent to give him more than she had ever given us. She made it clear that she would use this as an opportunity to right all of her wrongs as a mother, and she would take good care of him. And because of this, I moved out of her way. Even though I was not old enough to rationalize all of the pros and cons to this arrangement, I was cognizant enough to know that what she would provide for him would be better than what I could give to him. I didn't have anything to give or even know what I should have given for that matter. But I did know that I had carried this life inside of me, and I loved him enough to let him go.

CHAPTER 4

Bees in the Trap

When you learn about your honey, you learn how to get what you want with it. Every girl has honey, but we don't all use it the right way. I was. At least, I thought I was.

I had more than my fair share of poverty, and that shit was for the birds. I recognized game early. I saw how the dope boys looked at me, and I was looking at them with hope and prosperity in my eyes too. Finally, I found some people who wanted more than food stamps and roach-infested houses. Finally, someone showed signs of ambition. It had always lived inside of me, but I didn't see it; now I was not only able to give it a name but also a face. And although our neighborhoods had plenty of dope boys, I was never drawn to the employees. All I ever wanted was a boss.

Contrary to what anyone might have thought of me, I was not only smart but I also had a keen sense of street smarts. I had that shit you can't teach. Them niggas loved that. They loved everything about me from the way that I looked to the fact that I didn't take shit from nobody.

I started dating R as soon as I completed high school. My mother didn't even know that I graduated from school early. I had no desire to walk across the stage for graduation; it was lame to me. I had already finished months before the graduation was to take place. I got a job as soon as I received my diploma. Yet another example of why parents should pay attention to their children. My mother believed that since I wasn't going to school each day, I had dropped out, and quietly, I let her think whatever the hell she wanted to while I spent my free time with R.

He was smooth. A ladies' man for sure. And even though I knew he had many women, I admittedly turned a blind eye. I was the youngest, and all of those other old hags were jealous of me. They had every reason to be. I knew what I brought to the table. I was a trophy piece and loyal as fuck. He knew it, and he treated me like royalty. My perspective began to change. I knew that life had more to offer, and I wanted to make sure that I got everything that I was owed. I was a beast in terms of my thought process. What I knew for sure was that I wasn't ever going to live with the roaches like I had at my grandmother's house. I knew that I deserved better. I felt like I was on top of that world. You might not believe it, but he brought me furs, designer shoes, and handbags, and we always ate at the finest restaurants. We were far removed from the poverty that I knew all too well. If you had asked me then, I would have told you that we living the glamorous life. You couldn't tell me shit.

Eventually, I moved in with R, and life was good. Sometimes I would ride with him to make runs or handle his business, and I liked the way he moved. He was a boss. I learned so much by just watching him. The other thing that made me cling to him even more was the level of respect that the streets had for him. We would ride down Gettysburg (a popular street in Dayton) with the top down, and everybody would show him so much love. We were local celebrities, and everyone knew that I had his heart. I began to not even care about the other old hags because I knew that I was number one. In my mind, we were a modern-day, black Bonnie and Clyde. Because I had learned so much from the hard streets of Dayton, I knew the codes. I knew the lingo, and I knew how to make transactions happen too. I would watch as he would move through the streets, and I observed that one of the reasons he was so well respected was because he did not allow people to take advantage of him. If you owed him money, you would pay one way or another. If you tried to steal from him, that was considered biting the hand that fed you. Never do that. He took no shit. And as his lady, I gave the streets hell as well. Loyalty was everything. And even today, I still believe in loyalty, although I am certain that my definition has evolved.

One particular day, he asked me to take a ride with him. I knew immediately that it wouldn't be a joy ride through the city when he would say it a certain way. I knew that it was business. I was down either way because inside I also felt like it was a sign of respect that he would include me in his business. I knew he recognized that I was sharp. The car ride was silent, and I could tell that he had something on his mind. Another thing that I learned was that the boys in the trap did not like to be interrogated. If you were smart, you would look, listen, and learn through keen observation. We rode in silence over to a home that I knew he did business out of.

When he exited the driver's side, he motioned for me to come in with him. Like I've said, I was down to ride with him and do whatever he needed me to, but this house resurrected memories of pain. Begrudgingly, I opened my door and got out. As we entered, the house reeked of cooked crack. The smell made me nauseated as it reminded me of all the times we had to endure the smell when my mother cooked and smoked it. It has a unique smell all its own. It's vile, grimy, and if you ever have to be exposed to its poisonous venom, you shall soon never forget. Transactions were made here twenty-four hours a day. Imagine if Starbucks was open twenty-four hours and you could buy your coffee and enjoy it at the coffee shop as soon as you purchased it. The concept of this house was the same. The only difference is that nobody dies for Starbucks. People were dying every day because of crack. But in my mind, that had nothing to do with me or us for that matter. All I could think about was that R had found a way to rescue me from starvation and a poverty-stricken life. I was never going back.

As I entered the door, I walked slowly into the house, closing the door behind me. R motioned for me to go to an empty room down a hallway and on the left. The smoke in the air made the walk down the hallway feel like an eternity. When I got to the room, I sat in an old chair because I damn sure was not about to sit on that nasty old bed. Only Jehovah knows what has gone down on that mattress. I sat there for like thirty minutes in silence. Even though I had a cell phone, it didn't have all the apps and games and social media that we have on our phones today. If you weren't calling someone, your phone had no other purpose. I remember thinking that the room had one extremely small window. The room was so mundane and hopeless. I could only imagine if someone sat in here smoking their worries away how things could only get worse. No hope. No glimmer of sunlight. No chance for freedom. No matter how much darkness I had seen, I never wanted to be like the crackheads in my family. Life with

R had shown me what I already knew: the world had more to offer, and I wanted it all.

Even though I couldn't bear the thought of using it, I got up to see if there was a bathroom nearby. I had been sitting in that room for so long, and I didn't think that I could hold it any longer. As soon as my hand touched the knob, I heard a gunshot. I jumped, and my hand released the knob. I had no idea what was going on. We could be getting robbed, somebody could be here to take R out—the possibilities engulfed me in fear.

I paced around the room looking for somewhere to hide. I tried to hide in the closet, but there was no room for me to fit in. I got down near the side of the bed closest to the window, and I called out for Jehovah to save me. My memory flashed back to all the times that my grandmother would call out, "Jehovah," in desperation. Her voice was both frightening and powerful. Even though I didn't speak, I screamed out inside my soul. I didn't want to die. I wanted to live. I couldn't bear the thought of dying here. I couldn't bear the thought of dying in a place that I believe took my mother from us. I could not die in a crack house. I couldn't die in a crack house. I remained silent in hopes that no one would find me in the room. I was hoping that R was alive. I was hoping that this was all one bad dream. As soon as my mind drifted to the thought of the white curtain that had given me peace in the midst of war, I heard the doorknob rattle. Someone was there. I peeked over the edge of the bed and watched as the doorknob slowly turned. I could see a shoe walking towards me. With terror in my heart I looked up, and it was R offering me a hand up. "Let's go," he said. I was so terrified that I was speechless. This wouldn't have been the time to ask questions, so I didn't. I glanced at him to see if he was injured and recognized that he was just as intact leaving the home as he was when we entered. He opened my car door and let me in, and I unlocked the door for him to enter into the driver's side. He crank the car up, put in drive, and we pulled off. He reached over and placed his hand on my thigh as he always did, and I held his hand as I always did. The car was filled with silence. And oddly enough, we never spoke of that day again.

As I think back, I was so caught up in our lifestyle that I never once thought to call the police or at the very least try to see if I could have helped someone. I was so foul and so tainted. The thought of anything interfering with my escape from poverty was not even a consideration. To this day, R and I have not spoken about that day at the crack house. But what I do know is that yet again Jehovah spared my life. I do know that things could have gone much differently as they often do in these situations. Jehovah kept me from my demise.

Life with R continued as I knew it. Our love was full throttle. He meant everything to me. The old hags weren't even something that I thought about anymore. As far as I was concerned, it was just him and I against the world.

We were now preparing to bring forth life together, and I was pregnant with my second child. And even though my son was the first life that my body had given breath to, this felt like the first time. Maybe because I was not under the stress and constraints that my mother had placed upon me. With R, the health and wealth of our child was of the utmost importance. R was laser focused on getting to the money, and I was laser focused on holding him down. I thought that we were building a legacy, and nothing could stand in the way of that. But when your house is built on lies, it is sure to crumble.

After our baby was born, I returned to our condo, and life was as it should be. Me, R, the baby—what could have been better? When I walked past my closet, all I could see was rows of new clothes with the tags intact. That was how you knew your life was on point. On a particular Wednesday, R headed to the store to pick up a few items for dinner. I walked towards the couch to sit with the baby until he returned. I heard a knock at the door and looked through the peephole. I recognized that the gentleman at the door was a maintenance man. I opened the door and asked if I could help him. He stated that he needed to come in a check my water heater. I thought nothing of it because I figured that he knew what needed to be done. I should have known that something was off when he asked me where the water heater was. If he was a regular maintenance man in our building, shouldn't he have known where the water heater was? I digress. He took a look in various rooms in an effort to locate the water heater, and I allowed him to do what he needed to do. After about twenty minutes, he came over to me as I held the baby and told me that he was finished and everything looked to be okay. I thanked him and opened the door for him to leave. I could not have been prepared for what would happen after he stepped across the threshold.

A minute after he left, I had walked back over to the couch with the baby and the door was smashed in. All I heard was shouting.

"Get on the fucking ground!"

"Get on the ground, lady!"

"Is anyone in here?!"

I screamed in terror with my newborn baby lying on the floor next to me. My face was buried in the carpet as I watched what appeared to be a never ending line of black boots walking through the condo. "Is anyone here, ma'am?"

"No," I yelled. "Why are you doing this? What is happening?"

We had been hit by the feds.

I screamed in disbelief as they ransacked our home. Although I knew exactly why we had been hit by the feds, there is something inside of you that still feels that people have no right to invade your home and your privacy in that way.

As the series of events continued to unfold, R was facing significant time in prison. I began to wonder what would become of me and our child. I began to question if I was strong enough to make it on my own. Although I had always found ways to make money, I also always kept a nigga around to pay the bills. The money I made was always the icing on the cake. It made me feel secure that I could earn money, but I never had to worry about anything when I was with R.

I prepared myself to hold him down. I wouldn't dream of abandoning him at a time like this, or so I thought. I later learned that R had gotten another girl pregnant at the same time as me and that their child was the exact same age as our daughter. What the hell? After the way I held this nigga down, I can't believe that I didn't notice. But remember, I did say that I started not to concern myself with the other women. I was only concerned about what he and I had, and my mistake was in seeing things through rose-colored glasses. I was so loyal to him, and I would have done anything for him. I recognized that what I did have was freedom. R kept the street code and didn't include me in any of his activities that were illegal.

I consulted a lawyer to initiate the process of fighting to salvage some of our belongings. When I tell you everything had been seized by the feds, I mean everything. We didn't have shit.

R tried to maintain contact with me, but his disloyalty began to take a toll, and what was once a deep appreciation for how well he had cared for me morphed into hatred. I was so angry with him for not being truthful with me. In retrospect, I was angry with him for being exactly who he was. Now ain't that fucked up? I was upset with R for being exactly who he had been all along. When I met him, he had several women. One huge mistake that women often make is believing that we can change people. People only change when it is their will. There is nothing that we can say or do to make people be who they are not, and even if they change temporarily, they will always be who they are. What I felt for R can best be described as war in my heart. I wanted nothing to do with him. When the lawyers advised me that I had to provide receipts for the transactions made as well as statements of income to prove that I could indeed pay for the belongings that had been seized by the feds, they also warned me that I was not choosing wisely by pursuing the material items and that my time would be best served rebuilding responsibly. What they really meant was that if I kept digging, I would find myself legally an accomplice to what R did to earn money for our family. Game recognized game, and I shut down the court proceedings. I also shut down my heart towards R and closed that chapter of my life. Quite frankly, he was dead to me. I declared war.

CHAPTER 5

ATL Shawty

A fter war, the battlefield clears and the smoke lifts. It is in those moments that we must decide our next strategic move.

I knew that I needed to begin writing a new chapter for my life. I needed a fresh start. With a baby in tow, I picked up the pieces and moved from Dayton, Ohio, to Atlanta, Georgia, or ATL as we call it in the South. I had nowhere to go, and I damn sure was not exploring the option of remaining in Dayton or going back to the broke-ass project mentality that I was so far removed from.

I had a cousin that lived in Atlanta. Let's just call him L. Like most of the men in my family, L was about his money.

He would do whatever he needed to do to get it too. During this time, a movie called ATL had just hit the big screens. The movie featured rapper TI and actress Lauren London. The movie showed so many elements that appealed to me from the skating to the glamorous life that reminded me a little of my life with R. The hustler in me recognized that Atlanta would be a hotspot for me to make shit happen.

With $200 and my daughter in tow, I bought a one-way ticket and never looked back. My mindset was goodbye and good riddance to Dayton.

When I moved to ATL, I became the definition of a jetsetter. I felt so empowered because I was making moves on my own. I have always been smart enough to maintain a job and streams of income even when I was much younger. I never wanted to fully rely on anyone else to make sure that I never stared poverty in the face again. Even still, I always kept a few niggas around who would grease my palms with cash. That's the game. And even though I knew how to get it for myself, I hadn't known life absent of a man to take care of things financially and to protect me.

When I touched down, I connected with L who schooled me to making money drops. Not only did he school me, but he also created a generous income source for me. I could make as much as $2,000 one way from doing a simple drop. I was cute, so the men working at the airport loved me, and I used my intuition to run money back and forth. No one ever suspected my hustle. I looked too innocent. But had they taken the chance to open my suitcase, they would have discovered that I was a boss bitch quite frankly. There has always been more to me than meets the eye.

My cousin L eventually encouraged me to get a job working for the airline. L was always strategizing to get to the paper and I paid close attention. He figured that I could accomplish even more as an insider. During that time, the airline maintained a training program that took hours to complete. To make matters worse, the program wasn't even guaranteed money. I did the math and determined that I had the potential to make more money over time if I worked for myself. I also realized that I was never meant to punch anybody's clock. After living with R and watching his hustle, I was used to fast, heavy money. I quit that airline shit; it was way too slow. As my drop game got stronger, I was clearing more money than I could spend. But most importantly, I loved the feeling of getting my own money. I was living life, and you couldn't tell me shit.

One day, a homegirl of mine and I went out to eat at a popular restaurant in the city. People in Atlanta can be so flashy. This guy approached me, and I noticed that he blended in well with the rest of the flash of the city. He wasn't my type at all. I really hadn't planned on giving him the time of day, but he spoke my language when he flashed his money. He began a conversation as all men usually do, but in closing, he asked for my phone number, and I politely told him that I had no intention of giving it to him. What he did next caught my attention. He began writing his number down digit by digit on one hundred dollar bills. Dollar Bill was my middle name. I had never seen someone do something like that. And while I don't really like flashy niggas, I had to give props where they were due. After he handed me his number in bills, I walked with him to his car. There were two women in the car, one of whom appeared older and the other could have potentially been his sister. Either way, I wasn't really concerned about them, but I did notice.

A few weeks later, my girlfriend who was with me at the restaurant asked me if I ever called, and I truly had no intention of doing so. As I stated before, he was not my type. She kept saying, "Girl, you should just call him. He gave you all that money; why wouldn't you call him?" Influenced by her excitement and mostly intrigued by the money, I decided to call and the rest is history, I officially began seeing O. His money seemed to be neverending. He never spared me from any of it. Whatever I wanted, I received it. O spoiled me like I had never been spoiled before and I liked it.

CHAPTER 6

Sin City

I may be a lot of things, but a bitch I am not.
   I guess everyone has their definition of a bitch, but mine is someone who backs down or stands in idle silence when they recognize injustices around them. I didn't inherit that gene. As Diddy would say, "No bitchassness over here."
   O decided that we would continue the celebration of my birthday with a trip to Vegas. When I say that I didn't have to buy anything, I mean it. O bought me clothes and shoes for the trip and more. One of my final surprises was tickets to the boxing match featuring Floyd Mayweather vs Carlos Baldomir Torrent. We had ringside seats. I never

said it out loud, but I couldn't help but smile inside when I thought of how far away I was from standing in the line for government-issued cheese and that disgusting powdered milk. I was thinking to myself, "Mama, we made it."

At the match, we sat next to boxer Sugar Shane Mosley, his father Jack Mosley and some of the most acclaimed celebrities. It didn't hurt that I could see Denzel Washington and Suge Knight from where we were sitting. O was into the glitz and the glam, and I was definitely no stranger to it. Before we attended the fight, he took me shopping again, and I couldn't help but wonder why he wanted me to wear the most revealing ensemble to the fight. But I did as he wished, and like most men, he couldn't handle the attention that I received from all the other men. It takes a very secure man to parade his woman around in such a highly trafficked atmosphere and he not be jealous of the unmerited attention, gasps, whispers, and drools of other men. I handled myself accordingly and made it clear that I was only there with him.

When we arrived, I met his friend Tee and his girlfriend Marissa. She and I instantly hit it off and learned that we shared the same birthday. We turned all the way up! It didn't take me long to notice that her boyfriend Tee and O were beyond flirtatious with other women. And being the strong minded woman that I have always been, game recognized game.

After the fight was over, O and his homeboy told us to take some money and go hang. Because of how disrespectful I felt they were, all I could think about was the good time that Marissa and I deserved to have.

When we returned, O was livid. The tension in the room was thicker than the smoke. Even then, I didn't recognize the turn of events that would unfold. He began ranting with insults calling us bitches and hoes. "Bitch you smell like you've been sucking dick," he said.

With all of his strength, he punched me, and I fell to the floor in disbelief. I had never been hit by a man. I was so shocked I sat there for a moment. The pain around my jawline made me recognize that what had happened was real and that this was not a bad dream. "Get your shit and get up outta here, hoe," he exclaimed. "You will leave here with what you came with." And even in the midst of the pain, he hadn't said shit. I got up from the floor, took off the dress that he had given me, and slipped on a robe from the hotel. I knew that I had enough money to go to one of the boutiques downstairs in the hotel lobby and buy something decent to wear. I also knew that I had enough money to get myself a flight and get the hell up out of Vegas. Up till this point, no nigga had ever put his hands on me, and I wasn't about to start accepting that shit now.

As I began to pull my shit together, he began to cry, profusely begging me to stay and apologizing. I witnessed a different side of him. He pleaded with me, and it caught me off guard. Something inside of me still held me in bondage about leaving R when he was down and out. I never forgave myself for kicking someone when they were down. I felt like my whole life I have been down and out and continuously kicked. In his moment of sorrow, I forgot about the pain that he had inflicted upon me and I immediately began to comfort him. My comfort led to affection and affection led to lust and lust led to sex. We held each other for the rest of the night, and he assured me that what had happened would never happen again. I believed him. And although we had arrived in Las Vegas as two individuals, we returned to Atlanta as a couple.

    I became more and more dependent upon O. He was controlling, but I didn't really mind that much. After learning of my cousin L's brutal murder, my lick was dry. I had no more money and no more protection in the city of Atlanta. O took care of everything. And for a while, things were normal. I didn't love him, but I brushed it off as my inability to love. I needed a place to stay, I needed someone to love me and to take care of my daughter. O was our only option.

    As soon as I moved in with him, I discovered that I was pregnant. What happened in Vegas had manifested in me carrying new life for the third time. And as beautiful as new life is, the violence that erupted in our home was the complete opposite. From broken knuckles to broken ribs, war encapsulated me. And when I thought that things couldn't get any worse, I learned just how many children he had from other women. With babies comes baby mamas. My independence was dwindling, and his expectations of me had changed drastically. He expected me to stay at home and keep all of his other children at the drop of a dime.

As time passed by, I began to dislike him for his ill treatment of me. One particular day, he was so enraged with violence that he hit me in front of my daughter and she charged towards him. Even then, surrounded by war, I knew that I could not allow her to be subjected to such violence. I maintained that I never wanted my children to experience life as I had. I owed it to them to change what they would be exposed to and ensure that love was the theme of their lives, not war.

It also became obvious that O didn't feel the same about me. I do believe that even men who are violent sometimes love the women who they are violent towards but O didn't love me. He instead believed that he owned me. My theory proved to be correct when he went out of town and I called him to let him know that we had been robbed. His demeanor was lackluster to say the least.

We were robbed, and he didn't even come home. I had my young daughter, our newborn together and we had been robbed and he did not feel it worthy enough to come home and check on us? I found that to be strange but very revealing. What we were doing was no longer love if it had ever been. What we were doing was war. From that moment on, I recognized that my battlefield was his pockets. I had him set up on several occasions. I would arrange for goons to come to the house and hit the safe. My gain would come from splitting the money with them.

At the time, I felt like this was my only defense that I had against O. He had caused me so much pain. These acts were random and non-violent, but as I have grown through the years, I have also recognized that to plot revenge was just another way to realize your own demise. But at the time, I felt more than justified.

CHAPTER 7

Blood, Sweat & Tears

When your soul is beaten out of you, your heart stops beating. I had been bludgeoned too many times to count, and I kept going back. After giving birth to our first child together, I felt trapped. People always ask why women stay when they are being abused, and for me, the answer was simple: I just didn't want to uproot my babies. I remember how disgusted I felt every time we had to move and change homes as a child, and I couldn't bear the thought of repeating the same cycle for my children. No matter what has happened to me in my life, I have always wanted to be the best mother possible, and I wasn't going to let the blood running down my forehead stand in the way of that.

I remember sitting and staring out of the window and recognizing the green grass in our neighbor's yard, and although that yard was just across the street, a short walk away, it looked like freedom. I needed freedom from this life. For as long as I can remember, I had never quite been free. There was always some circumstance standing in my way and holding me back, but this time, as I sat in the window with blood rolling down my face from his fists, it was because of my own doing. Sometimes, we forget our part in situations when things are going to hell in a handbasket. Sometimes, we don't accept our own shit. I chased money, plain and simple. I ran from poverty like a runaway slave into the arms of money, and for me, escaping poverty was freedom. That was a lie I told myself for so many years. I lived so foul for so long, and I justified it by labeling it as freedom. But this day, this warm blood dripping from my eyelash made me realize that money held me captive. Where the hell can I go with my babies in tow and no money? I couldn't make runs like I used to. My fast money options were dwindling by the day. After learning of my cousin L's brutal murder, I was overcome with sadness for many reasons. The details of his death were too harsh to even repeat. My sorrow was heavy. I felt sorry for my cousin and sorry for my kids. I felt sorry that I couldn't do anything to provide for them on my own. I felt sorry that I had to rely on this motherfucker to take care of us. But you know what? I never felt sorry for myself. I did this. I was here because of my fucked up decisions.

When that drop of blood fell from my eyelash to my lip, I realized that I too had the power to get me and my kids the hell up out of imprisonment and I began plotting to do just that.

When I say I packed our shit, I packed like Jehovah was at the door. I raced through the house grabbing everything that I could. I wasn't leaving anything within reach behind.

I had a girlfriend who loaned me her truck to escape. I got behind the wheel of that truck and never looked back. I had nowhere else to go, so I went home to Dayton. I had promised myself that I would never return to the place that caused me so much pain, and I didn't ever really want my children to see this side of my life. I believed that they deserved so much better.

The kids and I stayed there for a while and I felt some sense of freedom because we had escaped O. While I was at home, many of my family members gathered at my aunt's house for dinner. While we were there, I sat across from my little cousin who was 12 at the time. As we all engaged in conversation, my eyes became fixated on her. The more I looked at her, the more I recognized her. To the average person, she appeared to be a normal young girl but I recognized the pain in her eyes all too well.

My visual inspection would also lead my eyes towards her stomach and I recognized the firm bulge that was extended from her body. She was pregnant. I leaned across the table and asked her: "Mila, are you pregnant?" I called my aunt near and I told her "Mila is pregnant". Everyone swore up and down that I was crazy and wanted nothing to do with my revelation. "Mila, have you been fucking"?

She sat there in silence and fear and I recognized her. I knew that someone had been abusing her. I knew that she too had her innocence stolen from her. She had been robbed.

The fact that my family didn't notice this child sitting there in pain made me sick to my stomach. No one loved her enough to pay attention to her to notice that she had been taken advantage of? No one loved her enough to keep her safe? This was a pattern that had become prevalent in my family for many generations. All of the women had been plagued by sexual abuse, molestation and promiscuity. It hurt my heart so deeply that no one had loved her enough. It reminded me of how I felt and that no one had loved me enough. I couldn't stand the thought of being there and Mila's pregnancy was an instant reminder of why I desperately wanted to leave and never return. I knew that I had to come up with a plan to get me and my kids back out of there. It would be over my dead body that I allowed someone to touch any of my children in that way. I would not allow them to grow up as victims like I had.

O made a habit of calling and I refused to take his calls. Jaded from Mila and coming face to face with the pain that caused the whole in my heart eventually, led me to a conversation with him. He begged me to come back home to Atlanta. He promised that things would be different and that I would not have to hurt the way I had hurt before. He promised me that he would not hit me the way that he had if I would be willing to return. I didn't believe him.

One morning after making breakfast for the children, I stood staring out of the window in search of freedom. While there, I saw a car pull into the driveway but I didn't recognize it. The driver's side opened and a face appeared. It was O. He had come to get us. He helped me to pack all of our things and load them into the truck. And even though I knew that I probably shouldn't go, anywhere was better than Dayton.

When we returned, things were calm for about a week and they returned to the normal bouts of violence. But I didn't care, I knew that the alternative was Dayton. I couldn't have my kids grow up there. I also recognized that subjecting them to violence at the hands of O was not healthy either.

Upon our second child's first birthday, I was living on my own. I was paying my own bills—well actually, you know I had a few dudes on the side to kick in on some bills here and there, but I was independent. I couldn't bear the thought of fully relying on anyone except myself for the well-being of me or my kids ever again. I had been through hell and war, and I had the emotional and physical wounds to prove it.

We decided to host the party at my home at the pavilion, and we invited a host of friends and family. And of course, I invited him because I wanted for our son to have both his parents in the celebration of his life. The atmosphere was happy and uplifting. I actually looked out the window and saw the sun that morning. We were blessed.

As the party progressed, I saw O speaking with a babysitter that we had both agreed upon to help me with the children. She seemed to speak with him often. In my heart I knew that she told him about a guy friend who visited me the other day. She seemed to tell him everything. I would notice that he would be aware of our going and coming even though we no longer lived with him. Yet another example of him viewing me as his property. But I no longer cared, I had my own place and paid my own bills and it was none of his business. After their conversation ended, I glimpsed over and saw the look on his face. My heart immediately dropped because I knew that he was in the midst of one of his rampages. I had seen enough to recognize him in this element.

"Come here and let me talk to you for a minute," he said. I told him that I couldn't come then because I had to prepare some food for the party. He kept trying to get my attention to come to where he was, but I knew that if I got within his hand's reach, war would ensue.

My celebratory mentality had shifted, and I now walked around the party donning a fake smile in fear of what he would do to me. I had been so far removed from him in that respect, and I thought that I had positioned myself for him to never hurt me in that way again.

I felt so stupid because I realized that even though I was paying my own bills, this was still his house. As I raced through the party trying to avoid him and pretend that everything was okay, I had memories of all the times that he had dropped by. The unexpected knocks at the door and the many times that he was just in the neighborhood and wanted to see the kids. All of these instances made him feel like he still owned me. I was still property. Fuck.

I was in the clubhouse putting away some decorations when I felt him grab me. My heart fell to my feet because I knew that this was about to get bad. Unlike many, he had no shame in beating me down in front of other people. And as many people sat outside in attendance at the celebration of our child's first year of life, I knew that none of them could save me while he attempted to beat me to death. He dragged me by my hair to the elevator, and as usual, I screamed for help. I had been here before, but there was something different about this time. I couldn't help but feel like this story was not going to end well.

As we made it onto the elevator, I begged him to stop. He responded in kind and poured a bottle of Hennessy into my face. The sting from the alcohol in my eyes and into my nose was too much to bear; I felt like I was drowning. Just as I caught my breath, I heard the bell from the elevator and I knew that we had arrived to the floor of my condo. He commenced to dragging me by my hair as I was yelling and kicking and screaming. If you've ever watched the movie What's Love Got to Do with It where Ike drags Tina across the floor, you can see this clearly. My back burned from the carpet, and I remember asking God to help me. I stood up, and although I could not speak, I was pleading for Jehovah to spare my life. As I stood up, he punched me so hard that my vision was blurred. I don't remember much after that except the sight of his foot hovering over me and pounding down. He stomped me that day like I was a man. I thought that I was dead. I could feel myself slipping in and out of consciousness. I was tired and gasping for air. I could still hear voices speaking over me.

His mother burst into the condo, and I heard her yelling for him to stop. He didn't stop stomping me until she ran over and grabbed his arm. She might have been the only one who could have saved my life on this day. I don't think that he would have stopped for anyone else. I know he wouldn't have.

When your will to live trumps your will to die, breath will find you.

As she grabbed him, I got up and ran as fast as I could. I had no idea where I was going, but I knew that this would be my only chance to save my life. For a moment, I thought of my kids, but I knew that they were safer than me, and if I didn't find a way to escape, they wouldn't have a mother to protect them. I couldn't bear the thought of leaving them behind in this kind of hell. They would end up like me or worse. I had to live. I had to survive.

I ran onto the elevator and pushed G for the ground level. When I got to the bottom floor, my friend was waiting there with her car running. "Come on, T. Get in the car."

I ran as fast as I could across the parking lot to the passenger's side. Some of his family members were standing near the entrance and had my children with them. I grabbed them in haste and loaded them into her car as fast as I could.

"Come on, T. He is behind you." How in the hell? He must have chased me out of the building. I remember her four-door, silver Honda because as soon as I got into the passenger's side, she panicked to lock the doors. She was shaking and he was banging on the glass with so much rage that her niece and my children in the backseat began to cry.

Her hand was shaking as she attempted to move the gear from park into drive. He was pounding on the window. I will never forget the look in his eyes: he intended to kill me, and he was enraged that he did not. With no strength left to fight, I again whispered, "God, help me."

My friend was screaming, and the children were yelling. The pounding on the car had us all terrified. With amplified rage, he pounded and shattered the passenger's window. I closed my eyes for only a second and felt the shift of the car in forward motion. She mashed the gas so hard that the tires screeched, and we almost crashed into another car pulling out of the lot in an effort to escape his terror. It seemed like everything was moving rapidly. "T, you can't stay with him. I can't believe this. It's too much. T, you have to leave him." She was so upset and began to cry. And even though she never spoke the words, she knew that had I not gotten in her truck, she would have never seen me alive again.

She had coordinated with one of our friends to transport me to a hotel. This friend had given me money before, but he was different from the others. When he gave me money, it had nothing to do with sex or even intimacy; he would give me money to genuinely help me. Almost like a father figure, I know now that he saw something in me that made him want me to reach my full potential. He reserved a hotel room for my kids and me and told me that he would pay for us to stay a few weeks. They had also arranged for me to get Pampers for the babies and some food. I kept rubbing my eyes and coughing from the Hennessey that my baby's father attempted to drown me with. I didn't have my contacts because I had rubbed them out from the burning sensation.

But none of this help came without obligation. He told me that I had a responsibility to make something happen, and he preached to me about my potential. I know that I was not really trying to hear what he had to say, but boy did I need it. I needed to believe that this was not the life that God had planned for me. I needed to believe that I was not living just to experience war. I needed to experience love. I needed the sun to shine in my life. I really wasn't sure how much more rain I could take. But as they say, even roses need rain, right?

I would later find out that my children's father had been picked up by the police on domestic violence charges. Even if I had decided to drop the charges, I couldn't have because the state picked up the case. They also charged him with child cruelty and terroristic threats for his endangerment of the children. A little later in the evening, I returned, escorted by police to the home to attempt to collect what I could of our belongings. The condo was defaced. He had shattered every picture frame and ripped my head off of every picture in the home. Everything was broken and destroyed. There was nothing left for me to salvage. I had shed so many tears that I couldn't even bring myself to cry. I knew that this meant that, once again, I would have to start my life from scratch. I came to him with nothing, and as fate would have it, I left with nothing.

CHAPTER 8

Born Again

I knew that God loved me, and that's why I never died. I should have been dead or at the very least in jail, but God has always had his hand on me. God has always spared my life. And even though I recognized that many of my trials and tribulations were at my own hands for choices that I made in vain, I have never let go of God's hand. I never allowed God to let go of mine. I remember how hard my grandmother would pray, and I watched the passion in her hands when she lifted them up to Jehovah. Even in the hellhole and amidst poverty, she believed in his power. Her prayers have kept our family. Even when my mother was strung out on crack, I believe that my grandmother's prayers kept her. Even when I swallowed that quarter in the front seat of my mother's car when she was inside that house smoking crack. And even when I was in the house with R when I heard that gunshot, the prayers of my grandmother kept me. I believe that we are all still here because of the prayers of those who have come before us. I don't take them for granted.

With a stronger spiritual perspective and no one else to lean on, I began to grind. No matter how I had gotten money in the past, I was not a stranger to grinding. Some people crumble up and die when life looks like an uphill battle, but me, I get ready for war.

I couldn't be on the scene because I did not have any of the materialistic things that I once had in the past. In Atlanta, depending on the circles that you run in, you are not accepted unless you have a certain status. I had a 2009 Dodge Intrepid which was a gift from a guy friend to get me back on my feet. And while I appreciated the car, it was not what I was used to. I increasingly saw how hard it was to take care of the kids on my limited budget.

I ended up getting a job at a bank and became serious about educating myself. An attorney friend would give me jobs doing office management. He would help me and allow me to do legal research and learn a lot about corporate and legal systems. Thus, I positioned myself to work in corporate America. I also kept my jobs at the club. I went from making $150 extra a week to $1500 by bottle waitressing and bartending. Most of the street guys knew me. No matter how many jobs I worked, it was hard. I used to never cry, but I would find myself kneeling and crying out to God because I felt like I was losing it. Before, I wasn't sure if I could hold it all together because of the constant abuse. I now wasn't sure if I could hold it all together because I was alone trying to raise my children. My days were long and always the same. My days would consist of going from daycare to work and back home to cook only to wake up and repeat. It felt like the weight of the world was on my shoulders. As a full-time mom working two full-time jobs, I never had time to sit and think let alone time to shower. It was so hard. The harder life got, the deeper in my faith I resolved to be. I recognized that the only way that I would make it was to sit down and make a schedule and have faith in God.

My reality was that I had four kids from three different fathers, and I was alone. These were the facts. I didn't feel sorry for myself; I felt sorry for my kids. I never wanted them to grow up in a home without a father like I did. I recognized that my children's fathers not being in their lives was not something that I could control, but the life that I created for them, I could.

I couldn't get the images of my children's faces out of my head, I lived for them. I didn't want them to suffer because of bad decisions that I had made. Some people blame others or their circumstances for what happens in their lives, but I

TIA BECCA

have always understood that a lot of what has happened to me was by my own hands. I dated the dope boys because I wanted to escape poverty, plain and simple, and while I'm not proud of it, that is my truth.

CHAPTER 9

The Lily of the Valley

When you run out of diapers and you don't have money to buy more, you recognize that shit just got real. As a single mother with four children living paycheck to paycheck, struggling to make ends meet, your sanity is an afterthought. There were days that I found myself sinking deeper and deeper into the valley. My spirit resurrected those same feelings of emptiness, and the sun refused to shine—at least it didn't shine on me. I found myself making baby food and trying to keep the kids on track. I got cut off from food stamps even though I barely had enough money to feed the kids and myself.

Fame and fortune is attractive, but when you are in the midst of the struggle, it's downright ugly. During those ugly times, I found out exactly who my friends were. I had no help. I remember being rejected after asking a (so-called) friend to watch my children so that I could have a little moment for myself. People would say things like "She need to have her ass home with all them damn kids" or "Who does she think is going to watch that many kids?" These sentiments hurt me deeply because I had been so giving to those same people when I had more. I would take my friends shopping with me, and if I had VIP status at the club, I would ensure that they had it too. These hoes lived the life because of my generosity; that was who I was. I didn't have shit to share growing up, so when I did have it, I always took great pride in spreading the wealth. That's why I don't really fuck with people now. My heart has hardened at the prospect of people really being there for each other. I can dismiss someone from my life without a second thought. I don't need anyone except my kids. I honestly still have a very hard time trusting people. And because of the hurt and the countless deaths that I have seen, I don't ever really cry anymore. I'm working on it though because my heart wants to believe that there are still good people in the world, but they damn sure were not there for me.

I was only twenty-five and even though I had four children, I still wanted to do the things that twenty-five-year-olds

do. You can't imagine what it felt like to go from and even
Even through the haze of life, one thing was painfully clear: I could only count on myself in this world, and that was it.

In these moments of truth, the dwindling amount of free time suffocated the life out of me. I was dying a slow death, and no one noticed or cared. Consumed with depression, I found myself questioning life and if I had the strength to make it. I questioned ever having children and even their existence. As ugly as it sounds, it is my truth. I know that I am not the only mother who felt like she wanted to give up. I know that I am not the only mother who felt life and sanity slipping through her hands. I was desperate for relief. I was a volcano waiting to erupt. I had never really learned how to be a parent. I had so many children, and I wasn't that strict, so many of the rules that I tried to enforce did not stick. As chaotic as my life had been in the past, I thrived off of order, and it was nowhere to be found. One of my babies loved to take off his diaper and pee on the floor, and I was tired and disgusted. From finding poop on the walls to disobedience, I was slowly slipping away. I was working so much that I felt like my children had no respect for what I was trying to teach them. Oddly enough, in my lowest moments, I reflected back to how much we resented my biological mother for never being around when she was working. It makes you really question how much history repeats itself. I had fought so hard to not become her, but when I looked in the mirror, she was who I saw. I could stand in the mirror for minutes that felt like hours and not even recognize the reflection. I had lost everything about myself.

No matter how low in the valley I felt, I have always believed in strategy. As much as I wanted to let life slip through my hands, I couldn't be consumed. I had to live for my children. The thought of them dealing with the abandonment that became ingrained in my heart was enough for me to fight. I hired someone to help me. I knew that if I was paying someone, they couldn't talk about me like them hoes did in the past. All I could think was that if I'm paying you, there ain't shit that you can say about me or how I handle my business or raise my kids. My grind became relentless. I restored order in my home. I began to write everything down and create calendars for myself and my children's activities. Organization was key and the solution to my OCD, the disorder that had taken me so low into the valley.

The most important area of my life that I exercised was my faith. I began frequenting The Kingdom Hall as often as I could just to get in a space that would allow me to pray. My faith allowed me to see beyond the darkness. My faith reinstated an innovative new train of thought. I began to recognize just how much I was in control and that I had the power to bring the order to my family that I had desperately been missing. As my heart started to heal, I recognized the value in my actions. My actions were the only thing that I had control over. I began to treat people better than they treated me. It was the best revenge.

When I focused less on others and adopted a laser-like focus for what I wanted to manifest in my children's life and my life, even my karma changed. Every time I worried, I prayed, and every time I prayed, Jehovah would send me a sign. Through my prayers, I promised that I would never date another man for money. My faith and my word was tested so many times. I would work so hard to just to make ends meet. When I was with the dope boys, money was disposable. Along the way, Jehovah never left my side. Sometimes, I would cry out and be tempted to return to what was comfortable, and God would send me a sign. An extension on a bill or a small bonus to get me by. I remained faithful. The jobs that I attained were better and better each time and allowed me to take steps towards upward mobility for my children and me. I had discovered that my power was in Jehovah and that, with my faith, anything was possible. I knew that I was stepping into new territory when I went to the bank to apply for a loan and the loan officer began to teach me about the importance of credit. She gave me tips on ways to improve my credit score, and I began to repair my credit and my heart simultaneously. With a new outlook on life, I would never allow myself to look backwards; I was no longer headed in that direction. At least I thought I wasn't.

CHAPTER 10

My Own Flesh & Blood

Sometimes you relive the past and you don't even know it because it is disguised as the future. It cost me $2,000 to kill my child, and I paid it. I had gotten pregnant again and could not bear the thought of giving birth to another child.

I know it doesn't sound like something that a sane mother would say. But as I have told you many times, I believe in telling the whole truth or nothing at all. You can judge, you can act like you don't understand, but this is my story; fuck what anyone has to say about it. It's my truth.

During what I felt like was the lowest point of my life, I couldn't bear the thought of bringing another child into this world. I was already at my breaking point when I met E. I found friendship and comfort in him.

I had known him for quite some time. Truth be told, he dated one of my friends many years prior. I thought he was cool, but there was something about him that made me know that things between us would never work. But sometimes friends turn into lovers, and that was the case with us.

I began to fall for him because of the way that he treated my children. I guess his presence allowed me to feel the very thing that I had searched for in my life and for my children: fatherhood. His presence allowed me to believe that I could actually have the family that I had always secretly searched for. Together, we played house, and I allowed myself to get pregnant by him. But no matter how much this looked like a happy ending, my body could not be the vessel for new life. I had no strength left to give in that respect, and I decided to terminate the pregnancy. Everything about the way that I handled it was deceitful. I convinced one of my girlfriends to take me to the abortion clinic and lied to him about my whereabouts. I had reached a new low when I faked a miscarriage. In true Tia fashion, I couldn't live a lie and eventually revealed to him that I had been the cause of our child's death. I had killed our baby at six months. It was murder.

Around the same time, E had tragically lost his brother to senseless violence of the streets. I would later learn that somehow his heart and his mind correlated our unborn child with the spirit of his brother. He had placed so much hope into the new life that we would bring forth. I just couldn't have found the strength to carry the pregnancy to term. His sentiment towards me went from love and hope to feelings of loss and hate. Things were much different, and we were disconnected.

The never-ending arguments morphed into lustful moments, and I was pregnant again almost immediately after the abortion. Although it may sound strange, I thought that I could right my wrong by offering my body once more as a sacrifice. I never wanted to be the cause of anyone else's pain. I had been at the mercy of people who inflicted great pain upon me all my life, and I could not stomach the thought of doing that to someone else. I can't exactly say that things were ever the same though.

While I was pregnant for the second time from E, we had a heart-to-heart talk. During that talk, E solemnly expressed that he did not want to be with me. He went into explicit detail about how his family felt that he could do better by finding someone who did not have as many children as me. They felt that my baggage would weigh him down. He expressed how his family would taunt him by saying things like "While you are over there playing house with her and trying to be a father to all her damn kids, you don't even spend time with your own nieces and nephews." And while there may have been truth in that we were indeed making what I thought was a life together, in my humble opinion, if a man dates a woman with kids, he assumes responsibility for what she brings to the table. What kind of sick, twisted mindset would allow you to think otherwise? At the end of the day, I'm still a G. I'm still a loyal person, and the same codes of the streets that I was raised on were fair game. Loyalty over everything. Or so I thought. No matter what has happened to me in my life, I have always accepted people for who they are and where they were in life. I prefer to let God do the judging. How can we be so judgmental when we all have pasts? Every single one of us.

When he told me his true feelings, it cut me deep in my soul. This pain that I felt even trumped those grueling days of laying in the bed next to my sister waiting for my turn to be molested. This pain hurt me in a place that even rejection from my birth mother hadn't touched. I couldn't figure out why it hurt me so badly, but it did. Not even the bludgeoned nights with O could top the rejection that overtook my spirit.

On that night, for the first time, I cried. The tears that rolled down my face felt like fire.

I wasn't mad because of how much I loved him; I was hurt because I had allowed him to take me to a place of vulnerability. I never loved any man enough to be heartbroken. I did not have the capacity to love that deeply, but this shit hurt me so badly. The hope of a woman is a powerful thing. I had hoped that E and I would create a life together. I had hoped that E would be a father to the rest of my children. I had hoped that E would be my down-ass friend and lover that wouldn't leave like the others, but on this night, my world came crashing down. I had given this man my body to bring forth new life to mend his broken heart, and this was the thanks that I received.

When you put everything into perspective, men play with the hope of women day in and day out. We invest so much into relationships that don't make sense, but our heart maintains hope that we will get what we believe we deserve. Admittedly, I was heartbroken. I was heartbroken not because I loved E; I was heartbroken because my hope was shattered. As I reflect, I believe that I had been kicked while I was down. I remember thinking about how I had kicked R when he was down, and I always said that I would never do that to anyone again.

But this time, karma had bitten me in the ass. I was already at the lowest point regarding my value for myself. The kids, the loneliness, and the pain from my past life had collectively taken a tremendous toll on me. While E spoke his truth, the rejection pierced my spirit like a sword. There I stood simultaneously pumping blood through my veins overtime for the life that was living within me and dying at the same time. The child that I now carried inside of me was not enough. I was not enough. But even in my broken state, I was still a G. When life has hardened you, moving on becomes second nature. Mutually, we agreed to separate and work to at least be friends for the baby's sake.

I fought to keep my sanity once again and protect the baby growing inside my body as well as the livelihood of my kids. It never mattered what happened to me, but I refused to not remain consistent in my efforts to keep their lives forwardly progressing.

After the baby was born, I still saw all of the qualities in E that I had most admired. He was an amazing father. Regardless of anything that I can ever say about him, I could never discredit him for being a good man and a good father. We found great success as co-parents. Knowing deep in my heart that E was never truly who I was supposed to be with, I was so thankful that my son could have his father in his life. This would prove to be such a positive influence, and I wanted that so desperately for all of my children, but this time I was successful.

After living apart, I began to find my voice and recognize my value. Many of E's shortcomings would be revealed too. I heard from a mutual friend that E and some of his family members brutalized one of their uncles and packed his body into the trunk of the car. While driving, they were pulled over and the police discovered the uncle in the trunk. Ain't that fucked up? E was hood—don't get it twisted—but like many niggas in the hood, they were good dudes who got caught up in lives of destruction. That's what the street teaches you, and that same fake love from the streets is the same love that will land your ass in jail. It's the same love that left me abandoned after I tried to get my life in order and no one was there to lend me a helping hand. That shit is for the birds.

Freedom began to slip through E's hands. The police were all over him. He was a wanted man. And when your loyalty rests in the streets, the sun will cease to shine and the storm will find you.

I made the decision to help E hide. Even after all of the progress that I had made and the countless efforts to erase this lifestyle from my existence, I was back in this shit again. That street mentality that had been ingrained in my psyche wouldn't allow me to let E do this alone. Even after he had kicked me while I was down, I couldn't respond in kind. Before I knew it, my mindset was foul. I was going to protect E at all costs. I went from struggling with the prospect of heartbreak to getting hotels in my name, hiding this nigga in my home, renting cars, and anything else that I could do to help him evade capture. We lived life on the low. And I kept everything in order with my kids' lives as well. They had no idea what was going on around them, and that is exactly how I wanted to keep it. I wanted E to be available to our child. My love for their relationship meant more to me than the consequences of my actions. I wanted to change, but for some reason, when you are in the midst of your shit, you will find so many ways to justify your actions.

After taking our baby to his two-week checkup, I heard a familiar noise that frightened me to my core.

"Get down on the fucking ground!"

"Ma'am, get on the fucking floor!"

We were surrounded by the sketchy voices of operators and dispatching requests for backup. The static make me sick to my stomach. I had heard that sound before, and it was never good. It was the fucking feds. We were surrounded. I watched from the ground as they opened the trunk of my car and the shit was loaded. I was just as surprised as they were although I never changed facial expressions. The truck was filled with guns—rifles and semis. In that moment with my face plastered to the concrete and my newborn baby on the ground next to me, I again silently screamed out to Jehovah to help me. I had not kept my word about these types of niggas. This shit felt like déjà vu. Hadn't I already done this song and dance? Hadn't I already been lying next to a newborn baby only to be raided by the feds? Hadn't I learned anything? My mind was fucked up.

In some twisted thought process, I thought that because I had not relied on E to take care of me, I was somehow removed from his criminal activity. I thought that because I was living my life on a straight and narrow path, I was not truly associated with the criminal activity that anyone else decided to partake in. That's fucked up, right? I now realize the error of my ways, but I didn't realize that then.

Yet again, my involvement with this lifestyle cost me everything. I lost my home, was taken in for questioning, and missed a great deal of time at work.

What I knew for sure was that I couldn't keep expecting Jehovah to bail me out. I recognized that I kept putting one cup of poison down to drink from another. If I wanted something different for my life, I had to stop jeopardizing my chances. I still hadn't loved myself enough to remove myself from the danger that loomed on the horizon of illegal activity and bad company. How many more chances would I request of life before I would be forced to meet my fate of self-destruction?

CHAPTER 11

Not Easily Broken

I relocated with the children and picked up the broken pieces once again. One day, I walked outside of my condo and felt something warm upon my shoulders. It burned slightly but in a good way. I looked up to see what had touched me so warmly on my skin, and I recognized it as the sun. Maybe I had never really felt its touch, but today, I did. It illuminated the day, and the sky was a big open field for the sun to play. In that moment, I realized that I was bound, not broken. There is a big difference. Sometimes when things are broken, they are beyond repair; however, when something is bound, it only requires freedom as a solution. For all these years, I have been bound by feelings of abandonment, bound by sexual abuse, bound by insecurity, bound by poverty, bound by illegal activity, bound by domestic violence, bound by men, and bound by my own heart. On this day, for the first time in my life, I felt free. Nothing miraculous had happened, and there was no specific moment of clarity; I was just sick and tired of being sick and tired. I had allowed so much negativity into my life that I was plagued by it. Today, in this sunlight, I realized that I had the power to free myself. Furthermore, every time I searched for freedom in others, I always lost. Today, with the sunlight upon my shoulders, I declared myself to be a winner. I declared freedom over my own life.

From that day forward, I began taking steps to improve myself. I started by deciding what I wanted to happen in my life and who I wanted to be. My first big step in this direction was to remove my heart from the for-sale shelf. I could no longer be bought for any reason. I was no longer available to men. I honored the fact that I did not have the capacity to love anyone else until I first established the endurance that it would take to love myself.

With honoring myself also came the notion that I needed to honor my body.

Physical fitness became a way of life. I threw away my sorrow for a membership to the gym. I tossed out my bouts of depression and picked up healthy eating habits and meditation. I even went under the knife to have a tummy tuck, my breasts done, and a vaginal reconstructive procedure because my bladder could no longer sustain after bearing the burden of five children. While you may find this to be extreme, I did it all for me. I was responsible for my own evolution, and it felt so good. I liked who I was becoming.

The moment that I began to love myself, I too became a better mother and more peaceful in my disposition in the world. My pursuit of money even evolved.

I got tired of not having access to purchase the things that I needed for my family. I resolved to maintain my finances in a healthy way and to maintain good credit.

I am no longer bound nor am I easily broken, and I humbly recognize that the sun shines everyday if I look in the direction in which light abounds. We all have the power to see the sunlight even when life deals us cards that we don't know how to play.

Today, I am still evolving. There is so much that I want to do. I don't see myself as a victim; instead, I define triumph. My children are thriving, and they know without question that they are loved. I look and feel the best that I ever have because I am in a positive space. My relationships with friends are evolving, and I recognize that we all need people to help us along our journeys. The most important lesson that life has taught me is that we are not defined by our past. It is part of who we are, but we have the power to decide if it is to be a part of who we will be. My life was traveling down a path of destruction, and I simply changed the course. I don't know what the future holds for me, but

TIA BECCA

I do know who I want to be in it. I recognize my worth, and I wear my crown like a badge of honor. Not too long ago, I met a friend who always refers to me as Queen, and you know what, I am.

CHAPTER 12

My First Love

Love is just a word to some, but to me, it symbolizes life. I have searched my entire life for it. I didn't recognize love nor do I believe that I had the capacity to process it. Love was a foreign entity in my soul. And even in the midst of uncertainty, I had hoped for so long that love would fill my heart and that I would be able to one day recognize it by name. Over the years, I began to believe that my reality would be one in the absence of love. I believed that love would remain hidden and I a stranger to it.

I recognized that the greatest love has always lived inside of me. I have nurtured it and fed it with my thoughts. My actions, my thoughts, and my existence have all been a result of love. My first love was my firstborn son. No matter how foreign the idea of being a parent was to me at such a young age, I fought like hell to get him here safely. I sacrificed my body and my life for him. And even though I never believed that my bringing forth life could result in anything positive because of my immaturity, I now recognize my son as one of my greatest accomplishments. I am in awe of who he has become and the future that lies ahead for him. I will never be able to express what it felt like to be given the responsibility of nurturing what would be a gift to the world inside of me. Love lived inside of me. And because of him, I now recognize that he was my first love. Even before myself, my son was my first love. I also recognize that in spite of my shortcomings, I have protected him from the various failures that resulted from my negative decisions and, most importantly, I have protected him from allowing the hatred to consume him as it did me. Allowing my mother to be a parent to him and waiving my rights was heart wrenching, but it was also the ultimate sacrifice; I knew that with her, he would have a life that I was not capable of giving him because I had not yet discovered love.

There is not a day, hour, minute, or second that goes by that I don't have thoughts of his face and long to hear his voice. There is not an action that I take today without him in mind. I am infatuated with his success because I now recognize that if he allows himself to be consumed by love, so shall I. My first love has lived inside of me, and I will be eternally grateful for bringing forth life that represents the breaking of generational curses, life that represents prosperity, and life that represents love.

In learning to love myself, I learned that the love that I had for my first born son rests deep within my soul. It was in a place that even I did not have access to. I never learned how to love myself, so I never knew how to love him. This is no excuse, only my plea that one day he will see me for me and he will know that he is loved. His ability to discover love is my final plea.

Conclusion

Each time I treat someone better than they have treated me, I win. I have learned so many valuable lessons in my life, but the most important is that I have choices. We all do. The choices that I made in the past became the points of my pain. I now recognize that I have a choice to end the vicious cycles of sexual abuse, drug use, violence, and destruction that have haunted my family for so many years. I have a choice to change the way that I view people and the way that I view myself. I have a choice to make my own money and be completely responsible for supporting the children that I have brought into this world. I even have a choice to develop a long-lasting relationship with my firstborn son. I have the choice to fight every day to ensure that he never feels abandoned the way that I did and that he knows without question that even though my start was not the best, I will do everything in my power to finish strong with him. All these choices and more belong to me, and because I have the right to choose, I am powerful. We lose our power along the way, and we are either placed in situations or we place ourselves in situations that deplete our power. I will no longer walk that beaten path. My greatest gift has been recognizing that even in the midst of wrongdoing, bad choices, and turbulence in life, we can simply change the direction. For me, this has been the difference between life and death. Today, I choose to love. I am a work in progress, and I am not where I want to be, but I am not where I once was. I find great pleasure in knowing that I am striving to be the best example for my children and to create businesses that can sustain us all. I work relentlessly, but I make it just as much of a priority to spend quality time with my children.

We all have the armor that we need to put on to win the war, it is love. The greatest and most powerful gift that lives inside each of us is love. We must remember to share it freely, because it replenishes consistently.

War as I see it is beautiful. After the smoke from the guns clear, there is a silent place of peace that surpasses all understanding. This peace is where I found the essence of who I want to become. This peace, I believe, is what the world needs. This peace is the only thing that I aspire to.

I want others to see me, know my story, and be inspired to want more for themselves. I want every person to recognize their value and know that your past does not always determine your future. We have the power to create the life that we deserve to live, and we have the power to attract or reject the people and energy we don't want or need.

We must be aware of and responsible for our actions. Every time I lacked accountability for myself in the world, I failed, but every time I assumed full responsibility, the atmosphere shifted. Things fell into place. This is how life works. Triumph is the ultimate manifestation of love and war, but when our will to live and our will to love is greatest, we will win the war.

As I have told you, without question, men have had a lasting impact in my life. The most important lesson that I have garnered from it all was to love myself. Throughout the pages of the book, each of the men were referred to by an initial. They were W, A, R, L, O, V, and E.

When put together, these initials spell two of the greatest words to describe my journey: WAR and LOVE. No matter how many times my encounters with men gave rise to great warfare, the greatest sentiment that lives inside of my soul today is love. I am intentional in the way I love, who I give my love to, and the love I wish to receive. It took years of war for me to discover love. I don't believe that I was ever equipped to recognize it or allow it to breathe inside of me. I suffocated love because I didn't recognize it. And the sad part is that the whole time, all that I have ever been in search of was love. I think we all are. We must acknowledge that when we are separated or rejected from the very source in which our love was created (in my case, a parent), we encounter more hardships in finding it and reconciling the resources to replenish it to give it freely to others.

I never knew love. But today, instead of the dreary overcast, I see the sky for what it is. I recognize the beautiful blue hues, and I see the sun that refuses to dim its light. It is shining whether we see it or not. This is my new take on life. I now love myself enough to shine every day and with every opportunity given, and because I recognize my worth and my value, I will never allow anyone else's to dim my light.

My story is very personal, and I have never shared the intricate details with anyone the way that I have shared with you, but I know that there is someone out there who needs to read this. I know that as women, we dim our lights every day for men who don't deserve our sunshine to begin with. I know that there is someone reading this who is in the midst of an abusive relationship and trying to make a determination as to whether or not to leave. I know that there is someone reading this who is afraid to leave the dope boys alone and learn to stand on her own two feet to earn her own money and not be a possession to anyone. I know that someone is reading this who feels imprisoned by their past mistakes. These are all examples of war. But love—love is the most powerful sentiment that we can bear. And even when we can't see it, it is ever present. Love reminds us to have the courage to try. Love reminds us that we deserve to be treated like queens. Love keeps us sane when we lose our way. Love, self-love that is, is the only way to win the war.

My name is Tia Becca, and although this is no ordinary love, this is my truth.

About the Author

Tia Becca is a mother, television personality, author, entrepreneur, actress, celebration specialist, inspirer, SHEro, and a survivor. She is on a mission to share her triumphant journey with the world so that people may be inspired to overcome and find the will to love themselves again. To learn more about Tia Becca, visit www.tiabecca.com.

Connect with Tia Becca on the following social media outlets:

Instagram: @tia_becca_
Snapchat: @tia_becca
Twitter: @tia_becca_

www.ingramcontent.com/pod-product-compliance
Lightning Source LLC
Chambersburg PA
CBHW070543300426
44113CB00011B/1777